FIVE EVIDENCE-INFORMED STEPS TO REGAIN CLARITY, REBUILD CONFIDENCE, AND LIVE WITH PURPOSE

The POWER of 5

OVERCOMING LIFE'S BIGGEST CHALLENGES TO THRIVE

Evelyn O'Donoghue *and* Donna Green

CONTENTS

THE 5 CORE CHALLENGES

DEDICATION

To the ones who keep going.
To those who ask deeper questions.
To every person who has ever wondered if they're enough.

You are.

This is for you.

ACKNOWLEDGMENTS

To the clients, mentors, and friends who shared their stories with us: thank you for your vulnerability, your courage, and your trust.

To our families, who held space for us while we wrote this thank you for your patience, love, and belief in our work.

To the practitioners, therapists, and researchers whose work paved the way: we stand on your shoulders.

To our early readers and inner circle you know who you are thank you for your honest feedback and unwavering support.

We couldn't have done this without you.

With love and deep gratitude,

Evelyn & Donna

ABOUT THE AUTHORS

Evelyn O'Donoghue, MSc, is a strategic business coach, wellness and grief specialist, and academic. She is the founder of Purisoul Wellbeing and holds a Master's in Information Systems Management from the University of Galway, Ireland. A Senior Fellow of the Higher Education Academy (UK), Evelyn is also a certified PRINCE2® Project Manager, Health & Wellness Coach (Real Balance), and Stott Pilates® Instructor. She combines structure with insight—blending emotional intelligence and practical strategy—to help business owners, leaders, and creatives achieve clarity, direction, and sustainable success without burnout.

Donna Green, Health & Wellness Coach, holds a Master's in Counseling and has over two decades of experience supporting individuals through emotional challenges. As the founder of Harmony Wellness Coaching, she helps clients reconnect with their self-worth and build lasting resilience.

As a widow, sole parent, and self-employed professional, Donna brings not only academic expertise but also a lived understanding of navigating profound change. Her grounded, honest approach creates spaces where growth becomes possible—especially for those who've carried silent emotional burdens for years.

Together, Evelyn and Donna bring over four decades of combined experience in personal growth, coaching, and therapeutic work. They blend evidence-informed tools, reflective insight, and a structured path forward. Their shared belief is that moving through life's challenges doesn't mean starting over—it means integrating your experiences and stepping into a life that aligns with your values. Through their work, they invite readers to see life's biggest challenges as powerful invitations to thrive.

INTRODUCTION: SETTING THE STAGE

Most people walking through life today are carrying more than they show.

Behind achievements, polished appearances, and ambitious goals lie quiet questions:
Am I really enough?
Why do I still feel so disconnected?
Why does success still leave me empty sometimes?

If you're reading this, perhaps you've asked some of those questions too.

This book is for you—the driven professional, the caregiver, the creative mind, the one who's always showing up for everyone else while quietly carrying an unseen weight.
You may appear to have it all together, yet inside there might be uncertainty, unhealed experiences, or a quiet voice reminding you that something feels out of alignment.

That voice isn't wrong. It just hasn't had a roadmap until now.

WHY THE POWER OF 5?

Numbers carry meaning. Five feels human—simple enough to re-member, yet strong enough to create change.

We live with fives every day: five fingers, five senses… and now, five clear pathways to understand yourself and move forward.

We chose *The Power of 5* as our framework because simplicity breeds clarity. By focusing on just five key areas, we can take complex, often overwhelming emotional challenges and break them into practical, actionable steps that create real momentum.

Throughout this book, we'll walk through five core emotional challenges. For each one, we offer:

- 5 real tools that create change
- 5 strategies grounded in psychology and coaching
- A final 5-step roadmap to help you thrive

WHO THIS IS FOR

This is for the ambitious person who secretly wonders why they're still anxious, even after doing everything "right."

For the one who leads others but feels unseen.

For the overachiever who can't stop striving because proving their worth feels like the only way to be enough.

You might be a coach, executive, entrepreneur, creative, or caregiver but what you have in common is this:

You want more than surface level success or happiness.

You want to feel like you belong in your own life.

WHAT THIS BOOK OFFERS

This is not just another personal development book filled with motivational quotes and vague advice.

It's a practical, structured toolkit for turning inward and healing old wounds with intelligence, compassion, and courage.

Each chapter follows a four-part structure:

1. **Storytelling** - Creative Narrative
2. **Teaching & Insight** - Psychological frameworks and personal growth concepts
3. **Tools & Practices** - The five tools per challenge
4. **Workbook Exercises** - Journaling prompts, trackers, and reflections

WHAT THIS BOOK IS NOT

This book is not therapy, and it's not a replacement for professional mental health treatment.

It's also not filled with quick fixes or toxic positivity.

What it *is*, is a roadmap, one rooted in psychological insight, lived experience, and practical tools. It's designed to help you understand your patterns, explore your emotional landscape, and take supported, sustainable steps forward.

You don't have to do this work perfectly.
You don't have to do it alone.

But you *do* deserve a structure that meets you with compassion and invites you to become who you were always meant to be.

A GLIMPSE WITHIN: STORY SNIPPET

She didn't see it coming. One moment, she was presenting quarterly numbers in a team meeting.
The next, her voice cracked, and tears pooled in her eyes.

"I'm sorry," she whispered, gripping the edge of the table. "I just, I haven't been okay."

Around the table, stunned silence.

For years, she had pushed through. Excelled. Overperformed. But the pressure finally cracked the armor.
The room saw her outer success every day but no one saw her inner storm until it broke the surface.

This is who this book is for: the ones who carry it all silently, under the weight of perfection.
Those who know there's more to life than performance.
Those who long for clarity, connection, and ease not just excellence.

INTENTION SETTING

Take a moment now to breathe.

Inhale slowly through your nose for a count of 4.
Hold gently at the top for 4.
Exhale slowly out through your mouth for a count of 6.

Repeat this cycle two more times, allowing your body to soften with each breath.

Gently set an intention for your journey through these pages:

- What do you most need right now?
- What would you like to feel more of or less of as you move forward?

Jot down your answers. This is the beginning of your *Power of 5* journey.

Let's begin.

THE 5 CORE CHALLENGES

"The Power of Five"
Five Core Challenges That Shape Our Inner World

Use this framework to explore which challenge resonates most with your own experience—it may be one, or several, at different times.

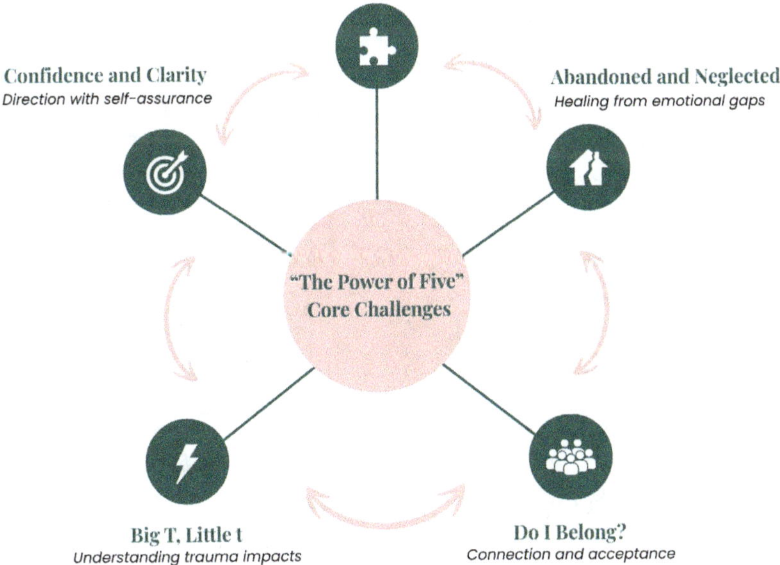

The 5 Core Challenges Framework (O'Donoghue & Green, 2025)

1

AM I ENOUGH?

OVERCOMING SELF-WORTH BLOCKS

EMMA AT THE CAFÉ

The whole café was filled with the comforting aroma of fresh espresso and cinnamon pastries, yet Emma sat quietly in the corner, sipping a glass of water. To anyone watching, she looked composed poised, even. But inside, she felt like a ghost.

The low hum of chatter and laughter swirled around her like vibrant brushstrokes on someone else's canvas, but none of it touched her.

She'd just come from a week filled with accolades: her team exceeded their quarterly target, her name was listed in the company's leadership newsletter, and she was asked to mentor new hires. Everyone said she was doing well, successful. But Emma felt like a fraud.

Her fingers traced the rim of the glass in slow, rhythmic circles, anchoring her in the swirl of self-doubt. *I'm not really that impressive. If they really knew me, they'd see I'm barely holding it together.*

The belief that she wasn't enough had been following her everywhere. It echoed in her head during high-stakes meetings, replayed in her mind when she looked in the mirror, and settled in her bones on nights when loneliness visited.

Dr. Patel, her therapist, had called it a *self-worth wound*. "You've confused being good with being worthy," she had said gently in their last session. "But Emma, worthiness isn't something you earn it's something you remember."

Still, remembering felt impossible. Every time she succeeded, her inner critic raised the bar. When she slowed down, guilt crept in. She didn't know how to rest without questioning her value.

That afternoon in the café, Emma opened her journal and wrote just five words:

I want to feel enough.

It was a beginning.

INSIGHT: UNDERSTANDING SELF-WORTH BLOCKS

Self-worth isn't the same as self-esteem.

Self-esteem often depends on how well we perform what we achieve, how we look, or what others think of us. Self-worth is deeper. It's the unshakable belief that we have value simply because we exist.

According to Dr. Brené Brown:

"You either walk inside your story and own it or you stand outside your story and hustle for your worthiness."

Many driven individuals carry invisible self-worth wounds. They seek validation through productivity, perfection, or service to others. These patterns often begin in childhood when love felt conditional, praise was rare, or emotional needs went unmet.

If we were praised only for achievements, we may grow up believing we're only valuable when we're productive.
If our emotions were dismissed, we may have learned to bury them along with our sense of inner value.

As Gabor Maté writes in *When the Body Says No*:

"The emotional self can be denied but not ignored."

These patterns don't disappear just because we become successful. In fact, they often intensify.

How This Shows Up:

- Overworking and burnout
- Inability to receive praise or rest without guilt
- People-pleasing or fear of saying no
- Constant comparison or imposter syndrome
- Shame spirals when we make mistakes

Awareness is the first step. But it's what we do next that matters.

THE POWER OF 5 TOOLS: RECLAIMING SELF-WORTH

1. Self-Worth Inventory

Write a list of five qualities you possess that have *nothing* to do with achievement.

Example prompts:
I am kind. I am insightful. I am generous.

This helps you connect to your identity beyond what you produce or accomplish.

2. Reframing Negative Beliefs "ANTs" (Automatic Negative Thoughts)

Identify a limiting belief (e.g., "I'm not enough"). Ask yourself:

- What evidence challenges this belief?
- Would I say this to a friend?

Reframe example: "I am learning, growing, and already worthy."

5-STEP COGNITIVE REFRAME TOOL

From automatic thoughts to grounded truths.

The Power of 5 (O'Donoghue & Green, 2025)

Cognitive Reframe: Step-by-Step

1. **Recognize**

   Pause and notice the negative thought or automatic belief as it arises.

   Example: "I'm not good enough to handle this."

2. **Challenge**

   Ask yourself: *Is this thought fact or assumption? Whose voice does it sound like?*

3. **Gather Evidence**

   Write down proof for and against the thought. Often, you'll find much more evidence against it than for it.

   Example: Times you've succeeded, praise you've received, goals you've achieved.

4. **Gain Perspective**

   Step back and ask: *If a friend shared this thought, what would I tell them?* This helps you soften harsh self-judgments.

5. **Replace with a Grounded Truth**
    Create a new, balanced statement rooted in reality and compassion.
    Example: "I've handled challenges before, and I'm capable of learning through this too."

Keep a Reframe Journal where you practice this process with one thought each day. Over time, it becomes automatic and weakens the grip of self-doubt.

3. Gratitude for Self-Practice

Each night, write down three things you appreciate about yourself that day.

Focus on how you *showed up*, not just what you *did*.

Tip: Keep small promises to yourself (e.g., "I will make my bed today") and acknowledge them aloud. This builds trust in your ability to follow through.

4. "Enough" Mantra & Morning Meditation

Begin each day with 4-4-6 breathing:
Inhale for 4 → Hold for 4 → Exhale for 6

While breathing, say:
"I am enough, as I am, right now."

Choose one empowering word each morning (e.g., "I am calm") and repeat it aloud three times. Let it anchor your energy for the day.

5. Boundary Mapping

Identify where you've been saying "yes" when you want to say "no."

Write one boundary you'll practice this week to protect your energy and honor your worth.

Boundary vs. Ultimatum:

- **Boundary:** "I will leave the room if yelling begins."
- **Ultimatum:** "If you don't stop yelling, I'm leaving you."

Boundaries are about **clarity**, not control. They help you protect your peace with calm strength.

WORKBOOK PROMPTS: RECLAIMING SELF-WORTH

Journal Prompt:
- *What was the first moment you felt you had to earn love or approval?*
- *Whose voice do you hear when you remember that feeling, is it truly yours?*

Worksheet Activity:
Reframe three beliefs you currently hold about your worth.
Reminder: No one knows you better than you.

BUILDING SELF ESTEEM & SELF WORTH

Chart of Experiences Shaping My Self-Esteem and Self-Worth

Why This Matters

- **Self-esteem** is how you feel about yourself in relation to what you do. It's shaped by external events and can rise or fall depending on circumstances.
  Example: "I feel good about myself because I did well."

- **Self-worth** is your inherent value simply for existing. It's more stable and not tied to achievements.
  Example: "I am valuable because I exist."

Exploring both helps you see how external experiences have shaped your self-esteem over time, and how your sense of self-worth has endured or evolved.

Year	Experience/ Event	Emotion Felt	Impact on Self-Esteem	Impact on Self-Worth
2005	Won first place in a school competition	Pride, excitement	Confidence boosted because of recognition and achievement	Felt valuable for what I *did*, but worth still tied to performance
2012	Failed an important exam	Shame, disappointment	Confidence dropped, felt "not smart enough"	Questioned my value beyond achievements, felt conditional self-worth
2016	Close friend moved away	Sadness, loneliness	Felt less socially confident without their presence	Realized I still mattered to others who stayed, began separating worth from circumstances

Your Turn: Chart Your Experiences

Use the blank chart below to reflect on your own key moments.
Include both positive and painful experiences.

Year	Experience/ Event	Emotion Felt	Impact on Self-Esteem	Impact on Self-Worth

How to Use the Chart

1. **Year** – Write the year the experience occurred.
2. **Experience/Event** – Briefly describe the significant event.
3. **Emotion Felt** – Write the emotions you felt at that time (e.g., pride, sadness, joy, fear).
4. **Impact on Self-Esteem** – Reflect on how this influenced your confidence or self-image at the time.
5. *Perceived* **Impact on Self-Worth** – Reflect on how you felt this event affected your deeper sense of being valuable. *(Note: your worth itself does not change, but it may have felt challenged or affirmed in that moment.)*

Think of this as your *personal map*. It shows when your self-esteem was boosted or challenged — and how your sense of self-worth may have felt shaken, affirmed, or grown more resilient over time.

REFLECTION: MOVING FORWARD

Self-worth doesn't come from the outside.
It's not handed to you by achievements, relationships, or praise.

It's something you nurture, remember, and reclaim from within, sometimes gently, sometimes through deep honesty.

Like Emma, your breakthrough doesn't need to be dramatic or loud.
It begins quietly.
It begins with truth.
It begins with the choice to believe perhaps for the first time that you are enough.

You do **not** need to earn your worth.
You don't need to wait until you're more "successful," "healed," or "perfect."

You already are someone worth respecting, loving, and listening to.

Let this be your starting point not a finish line.
Take a breath now. Write it down:

I am enough.
I deserve the life I desire.

Say it again tomorrow.
And the day after that.
Not because you need convincing but because repetition becomes reality.

You are not the person you used to be.

You're becoming someone rooted, aware, and more connected to yourself than ever before.

This is your beginning, too.

2

ABANDONED & NEGLECTED

HEALING WOUNDS OF DISCONNECTION

STORY: THE OVER-GIVER

At first glance, Mariah seemed like the glue that held her world together. She remembered birthdays, organized team lunches, volunteered to help friends move, and rarely missed a text.

But the truth was more complicated
Mariah was terrified of being forgotten.

Her life was filled with constant motion: checking in on everyone else, doing more than was asked, avoiding the stillness that made her feel invisible. Beneath her cheerful energy was a deep fear of being unwanted. The moment someone didn't reply to her message or a friend canceled dinner plans, that fear rushed in like a tidal wave:

Maybe they don't really care. Maybe I don't matter.

Mariah's earliest memories were of being left alone after school, her mother working long hours, her father absent. She never wanted to be a burden, so she learned to be "good." Helpful. Low-maintenance. But inside, she often felt like a forgotten child waiting to be noticed.

In therapy, she heard the term *emotional neglect* for the first time.

> "You weren't abandoned in the traditional sense," her therapist said gently, "but your needs weren't acknowledged and that leaves a mark."

Mariah nodded through tears.
She finally understood why silence hurt so much.

INSIGHT: UNDERSTANDING THE WOUNDS OF DISCONNECTION

Abandonment and neglect aren't always dramatic events. Sometimes, they're subtle absences:
The phone that never rings.
The parent who doesn't listen.
The feeling that no one really *sees* you.

As Dr. Thema Bryant writes:

> *"Healing means identifying the ways you adapted to survive and learning new ways to thrive."*

When these patterns begin in childhood, we often internalize the idea that our needs are *too much* or worse, that *we* are too much.

In Adulthood, Unhealed Disconnection May Look Like:

- Over-giving to prove you're worthy of love or loyalty
- Feeling uncomfortable or even ashamed when asking for help
- Believing you must handle everything alone
- Panicking when someone pulls away, even slightly
- Ignoring your own needs or self-care because it feels "selfish"

These responses aren't flaws.

They're survival strategies, adaptations developed when connection felt unsafe or inconsistent.

The tools in this chapter will help you begin the shift from survival to security gently, and at your own pace.

How This Shows Up:

- People-pleasing and over-functioning
- Fear of being a burden
- Constant worry about being left out or forgotten
- Struggles with trusting others
- Difficulty expressing your needs or emotions

THE POWER OF 5 TOOLS: REBUILDING CONNECTION AND INNER SAFETY

1. Circle of Trust Map

Identify 2 or 3 people who consistently show up for you with presence, honesty, and care.

CIRCLE OF TRUST MAP

Identify the Relationships That Support You

Professional Only
Strictly work/professional contacts

Acquaintances
People you know socially but don't share personal matters with

Outer Circle
Friends or extended family you share occasional updates with

Close Circle
People you trust with most personal matters

Inner Circle
People you trust completely (family, best friends)

CIRCLE OF TRUST – TEMPLATE
Identify the Relationships That Support You

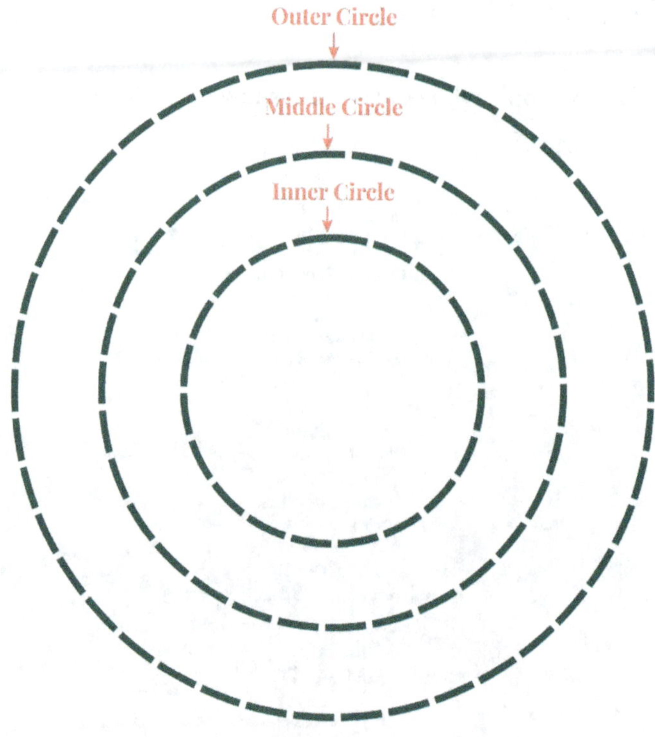

Instructions:
Inner Circle: Closest people you fully trust.
Middle Circle: People you trust in specific areas.
Outer Circle: Acquaintances or professionals you rely on
occasionally.
Write names or initials in the circles.

Reflection: What do these people have in common? What qualities make you feel safe and emotionally seen?

Use this map as a reminder:

You are not alone.

Safe connection *is* possible.

2. Inner Child Letter

Write a compassionate letter to your younger self from the perspective of your grounded, wise adult self.

- Acknowledge any pain, confusion, or unmet needs they carried.
- Offer comfort, validation, and a new narrative of safety.

Reminder: It's okay to feel lingering anger or grief toward caregivers, even if they "did their best."
You're not blaming you're releasing.
You are safe now.

3. Self-Soothing Toolkit

Create a personalized list of go-to comfort strategies to help regulate your nervous system when you feel anxious, disconnected, or overwhelmed.

Ideas to include:

- Deep belly breathing
- Calming music
- Warm tea or scent-based rituals
- Grounding textures (e.g., holding a stone or soft blanket)
- Nature walks or quiet, device-free moments outdoors

Keep your toolkit visible or accessible especially during high-stress days.

4. Boundaries & Reconnection Scripts

Practice communicating your needs with clarity and kindness. Boundaries create space for safety *and* reconnection.

Example Script:

> "I care about you, but I need to honor my energy right now. I'll reconnect when I feel more grounded."

Practice saying it out loud or write your own version. Boundaries are not rejection they are protection.

5. Daily Grounding Practice

Choose one small ritual that helps you feel centered and connected to yourself each day.

Example: Each morning, place your hand over your heart and ask:

> *"What do I need today?"*

This creates a consistent signal to your nervous system:
I am listening.
I am showing up for myself.

WORKBOOK PROMPTS

- **Journal Prompt:** *What memories come up when you feel forgotten or ignored?*
- **Exercise:** Create a "Safe Connection" list; who do you feel emotionally safe with, and why?

- **Reflection:** When do you over-give or stay silent to avoid disconnection?
- **Script Practice:** Write and rehearse one boundary-setting phrase.

REFLECTION: MOVING FORWARD

You are not too much.
Your needs are not a burden.
And you do not have to prove your worth through constant giving.

Healing from emotional neglect means learning that connection starts within. You can offer yourself the presence, kindness, and attunement you may have missed.

This isn't about cutting people out.
It's about *calling yourself back in.*

Breathe into the truth:
You are worthy of being seen and supported.

Let's keep going.

3

DO I BELONG?

NAVIGATING SOCIAL ANXIETY & FITTING IN

STORY: THE SILENT LEADER

Rachel was a rising star in her company. Sharp, articulate, and often the one with the best ideas in the room but almost no one knew it.

Meetings would come and go, and while others chimed in with half-formed thoughts, Rachel kept hers to herself.

She feared judgment.
Worse, she feared the silence after she spoke the awkward pause that might follow a misunderstood comment.

So she held her ideas close, nodding along even when she disagreed, secretly kicking herself afterward.

In school, Rachel had been bullied. Called "weird" or "too much," she learned early that standing out meant being picked apart. Over the years, she developed a careful social armor. She could be pleasant, agreeable, even warm but never too loud, too honest, or too present.

Her therapist once asked,

> "Do you want to be liked, or do you want to be known?"

The question haunted her.
Rachel didn't want to be invisible but she didn't know how to belong without shapeshifting.

That question became her turning point.

INSIGHT: BELONGING VS. BLENDING IN

We all want to belong. But many of us mistake belonging for approval. We think fitting in means being accepted but true belonging requires being seen.

For those who've faced bullying, exclusion, or rejection, the need to blend becomes a survival tactic. We become social chameleons, hiding parts of ourselves to stay safe.

But safety built on self-erasure isn't safety at all.

As Dr. Brené Brown writes:

> "True belonging doesn't require you to change who you are; it requires you to be who you are."

For driven people, social anxiety can look like quiet perfectionism. It's not always visible but it can be deeply painful.

Social anxiety isn't just about shyness. It's about the fear of being exposed misunderstood, dismissed, or excluded.

In Driven People, Social Anxiety Can Look Like:

- Holding back in groups
- Second-guessing what you said (or didn't say)
- Over-preparing for casual conversations
- Downplaying accomplishments

The journey to real belonging begins when we choose authenticity over acceptance.

How This Shows Up:

- Fear of speaking up
- Difficulty maintaining eye contact or making small talk
- Overanalyzing social interactions
- Exhaustion after group settings
- Feeling like an outsider, even among friends

THE POWER OF 5 TOOLS: REBUILDING SOCIAL CONFIDENCE

1. Belonging Statement

Write a personal affirmation that reflects true belonging. Example:

"I belong when I express myself with honesty and kindness."

Repeat it daily. Let it root into your nervous system as truth.

2. Social Resilience Post-Event Practice

After a social interaction, take a few moments to journal:

- What went well?
- What felt uncomfortable?
- What did I learn?

This builds self-awareness without self-criticism.

3. Micro-Exposure Confidence Tasks

Set small, weekly stretch goals:

- Ask one question in a meeting
- Attend a networking event
- Share a win online
- Give a compliment to someone you admire

These small acts of visibility build courage over time.

4. Values-Based Networking

Instead of focusing only on industry or status, engage in conversations and communities that align with your values.

When we connect over meaning not just metrics authenticity comes more naturally.

5. Rejection Reframing Journal

Revisit moments of social rejection and gently ask:

- What did I assume about myself or others?
- What else could be true?
- What's a more compassionate interpretation?

This practice rewires the narrative from shame to self-trust.

WORKBOOK PROMPTS

- **Journal:** When have you felt most like yourself in a group?
- **Exercise:** List 3 environments where you feel safe to be authentic.
- **Reflection:** What are you afraid might happen if you speak up?
- **Statement Practice:** Write and repeat your "I Belong" affirmation daily.

REFLECTION: MOVING FORWARD

You don't need to blend in to belong.
You don't need to be liked by everyone to be loved by the right people.
You don't need to hide the very parts of you that make you whole.

Belonging begins within.
And it grows every time you choose to show up as yourself.

Repeat after me:

I belong, because I am.

Let's keep going.

4

BIG T, LITTLE T

REFRAMING PAINFUL EXPERIENCES

STORY: THE NUMB ACHIEVER

Lauren's life was curated to perfection. She ran a successful business, had a beautiful apartment, and always had an answer for everything. But behind the poised exterior was a history of quiet suffering she rarely spoke of.

There had been big traumas, abuse in her early twenties, a sudden loss in her family. And there were the little traumas too, growing up in a house where emotions were met with silence, where vulnerability was dismissed as weakness.

Lauren carried her pain like a sealed box. She told herself she'd dealt with it, that it was "in the past."

But her body told a different story.
Anxiety pulsed through her chest when things got quiet.
She felt drained after client calls but couldn't explain why.
Some days, she felt nothing at all.

In therapy, her counselor introduced the idea of "Big T" and "little t" trauma. It helped her understand why certain memories still haunted her and why others, though seemingly minor, had shaped how she saw herself and the world.

"I always thought trauma meant something violent or catastrophic," Lauren admitted.
"But what if it's also the constant absence of safety?"

That question cracked something open.
For the first time, she allowed herself to feel to grieve what she had minimized for so long.

INSIGHT: UNDERSTANDING BIG T VS. LITTLE T TRAUMA

Trauma isn't solely defined by the event itself, but by its impact on the nervous system.

- **Big T trauma** refers to significant, often catastrophic events: abuse, sexual or physical assault, major accidents, chronic illness, or the death of a loved one.
- **Little t trauma** involves more subtle but often repeated experiences that are frequently overlooked: chronic criticism, emotional neglect, prolonged stress, or consistent exclusion.

Secondary or witness trauma can also leave lasting effects. (See Appendices A and B.)

All types of trauma whether "Big T" or "little t" shape the brain and body.
Both create survival patterns that may have once protected us, but now keep us stuck.

As Dr. Bessel van der Kolk writes in *The Body Keeps the Score*,

> "Unprocessed trauma isn't just a memory it's stored
> in the body."

It can manifest as physical tension, chronic health issues, emotional reactivity, or patterns of disconnection.

Reframing trauma means **naming it**, **making sense of it**, and learning how to support ourselves as we move forward not by erasing the past, but by changing how we live with it.

How This Shows Up:

- Hypervigilance or numbness
- Chronic anxiety or emotional shutdown
- Feeling out of control emotionally
- Avoidance of intimacy or vulnerability
- Exhaustion with no clear cause

THE POWER OF 5 TOOLS: REFRAMING AND SOOTHING TRAUMA RESPONSES

1. Trauma Triggers Map

Notice recurring emotional reactions that feel bigger than the moment.

Ask:

- "What does this remind me of?"
- "When did I first feel something similar?"

Tracing these patterns brings awareness so we can respond rather than react.

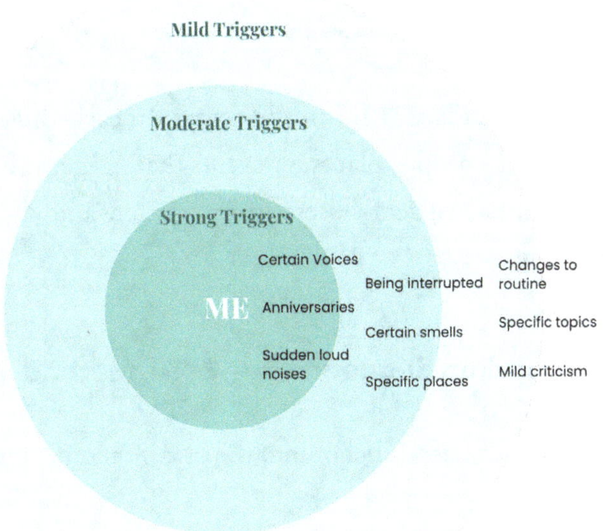

TRAUMA TRIGGERS – TEMPLATE
Mapping What Activates Your Stress Response

Mild Triggers
Add mild triggers (small stressors or discomforts)

Moderate Triggers
List moderate triggers (unsettling but manageable)

Strong Triggers
Note your strongest triggers (events, people, or reminders that
cause intense reactions)

ME

Reflect:
What patterns do I notice? Which triggers do I want to explore further?

Instruction: Place "Me" in the center. In each ring, write examples of situations, people, places, or events that trigger you—starting with the strongest triggers closest to the center, and the mildest in the outer ring.

2. Grounding Sequence 5-4-3-2-1 Method

When anxiety rises, anchor into the present moment with your senses:

- 5 things you can see
- 4 things you can feel
- 3 things you can hear

- 2 things you can smell
- 1 thing you can taste

This activates the parasympathetic nervous system and signals to your body: I am safe now.

3. Rewrite the Story Practice

Choose a painful memory that still carries emotional weight.

- First, write it in third person as if it happened to someone else.
- Then, rewrite the story through a lens of compassion and strength.

Focus on:

- What that version of you needed and deserved
- Your resilience
- How you survived

This doesn't erase the pain but it reclaims your power.

4. Somatic Tracking Exercise

Emotions live in the body.

- **Notice:** Where do you feel tension or numbness?
- Gently breathe into those areas with **4-4-6 breathing** (Inhale 4, hold 4, exhale 6).
- **Add light movement:** stretch, shake, or apply comforting touch.

This helps release stored emotion and restore calm.

5. Personalized Self-Care Plan

Create a Self-Support Kit tailored to you:

- **Daily rest rituals** (journaling, quiet time, nature)
- **Safe people** you can reach out to
- **Emergency grounding tools** (soothing objects, playlist, calming apps)
- **Comfort items** (favorite blanket, tea, book, scents)
- **Affirmations:**

"I am safe now."
"I deserve care and gentleness."
"My needs matter."

Keep it visible. Use it proactively, not just in crisis.

WORKBOOK PROMPTS

- **Journal:** What memory or experience do I downplay, but still feel in my body?
- **Exercise:** Create a "Resilience Timeline" of painful events *and* your responses.
- **Reflection:** What does *safety* feel like for me?
- **Body Scan:** Set a timer for 5 minutes and slowly notice each area of your body. What feels tight, relaxed, numb, or alive?

REFLECTION: MOVING FORWARD

You don't have to compare your pain to anyone else's to validate your experience.
Big or small if it hurt or overwhelmed you, it matters.

Trauma may have shaped part of your story, but it does not define your future.

Healing isn't about erasing the past.
It's about *reclaiming the present.*

With each breath, you soften.
With each choice, you return home to yourself.

Take a slow breath now.

Say gently to yourself:

> *I am safe now.*
> *In this moment, I am healing. I am here.*

Let's keep going.

5

CONFIDENCE & CLARITY

MOVING BEYOND EMOTIONAL HURDLES

STORY: THE COACH WHO DOUBTED

Ava was the kind of coach others admired.

Her clients thrived, her calendar was full, and her testimonials spoke of transformation. But behind the polished branding and public speaking gigs was a persistent sense of unease.

Before every client session, she rehearsed what she'd say. After every workshop, she dissected each moment.
Did they find that useful? Did I sound nervous? Should I have said more?

Despite her success, Ava felt like an imposter. Her decisions took hours. She changed her mind often. She compared herself to everyone online. Her business looked like a dream but it didn't feel like one.

In one particularly honest moment, Ava wrote in her journal:
I know what I'm doing. I just don't trust myself.

Her therapist's words echoed in her mind:
"Confidence isn't knowing you're always right. It's being okay when you're not."

That shifted everything. Ava didn't need perfection. She needed clarity and permission to trust herself again.

INSIGHT: CONFIDENCE ISN'T LOUD IT'S GROUNDED

Many driven people equate confidence with charisma, decisiveness, and being the most knowledgeable person in the room. But real confidence is quieter. It's the ability to take action even when doubt whispers in your ear.

Clarity comes when we stop outsourcing our validation and start trusting our internal compass. Confidence grows when we take small risks, survive the discomfort, and witness our own resilience.

Emotional hurdles often cloud our ability to make decisions or take aligned action. We second-guess, procrastinate, or overthink. The way forward isn't to "push harder" it's to pause, connect inward, and act with intention.

As Dr. Carol Dweck has shown in her research on growth mindset, the belief that we can learn and adapt is more powerful than innate certainty. Confidence is built in the doing.

How This Shows Up:

- Constantly changing your mind or delaying decisions.
- Overthinking every email, message, or conversation.
- Struggling to articulate your ideas or offers.
- Doubting your abilities despite positive feedback.
- Needing external validation to move forward.

THE POWER OF 5 TOOLS

1. Confidence Wins Tracker

Why This Matters

Building confidence is about noticing and celebrating small acts of courage, not just the big milestones. By tracking these wins, you strengthen both your self-esteem (feeling good about what you do) and your self-worth (remembering you are valuable simply for being you).

Exercise: Track Your Wins

Over the next week, record five small moments of courage or confidence. These don't have to be dramatic — they can be everyday actions that show you're stepping up, setting boundaries, or honouring yourself.

Date	Confidence Win	How I Felt	Impact on Self-Esteem	Reminder of My Self-Worth

Examples of Small Confidence Wins

- I spoke up in a meeting and shared my perspective.
- I said "no" to an extra commitment to protect my energy.
- I kept my promise to check my finances this week.
- I took my scheduled 15-minute walk despite a packed day.
- I made my bed every morning, starting each day with a win.
- I asked for help with the kids instead of doing everything myself.
- I celebrated completing a project instead of immediately moving to the next task.

At the end of the week, read through your wins. Notice how keeping promises to yourself—especially the small, daily ones—builds a foundation of self-trust. Each kept commitment, no matter how minor, reinforces that you are reliable to yourself and strengthens your confidence from the inside out.

2. Vision of Success Mapping

- Define what success looks like in this season of your life.
- Use categories like: relationships, health, business, energy, impact.

3. Boundary Practice Scripts

- Write and practice 3 scripts for saying no, making clear requests, or ending self-sabotaging patterns.
- Example: "I'm not available for that right now, but I'll circle back when I am."

4. Emotion-Awareness Flowchart

When overwhelmed, pause and ask:
- What am I feeling?
- What is this emotion asking me to notice?
- What would be the most self-honoring action right now?

5. Weekly Alignment Ritual

Choose a time to reflect:
- What felt good this week?
- Where did I compromise my clarity?
- What will I realign next week?

BUILDING TRUST IN YOURSELF: CONFIDENCE AND CLARITY EXERCISES

True confidence isn't built by doing more it's built by trusting yourself more.

Journal Prompt:
Where in my life do I feel most confident? Where do I feel least confident?

Notice any patterns between environments, people, or roles. Reflect on whether certain environments support or diminish your confidence and why.

Belief Reflection Exercise:

What beliefs are holding me back from trusting myself?

Ask yourself:

- Did this belief once serve me but no longer does?
- Is this truly my voice, or something I absorbed from others?
- Is this belief a fact, or a perception I've carried without questioning it?
- And is it serving me now?

This exercise helps you gently dismantle the inner critic and re-center your own truth.

Clarity Compass Mapping:

What is a Clarity Compass?

A Clarity Compass is a simple but powerful tool that helps you make decisions based on what matters most, your core values and personal vision.

It anchors you when external noise, fear, or pressure try to pull you off course.

Create your Clarity Compass:

1. Identify your top 5 core values (e.g., Integrity, Freedom, Growth, Compassion, Creativity).

2. Write a one-sentence vision of the life you want to build, rooted in those values.

3. Use your Clarity Compass when facing choices
   - *Does this align with what matters most to me?*
   - *Does this move me closer to the life I truly want?*

Example:

- Top Values: Integrity, Curiosity, Freedom, Connection, Growth
- Vision Statement: *I build a life rooted in curiosity and connection, where I grow freely and act with integrity every day.*

CLARITY COMPASS

Anchor Your Choices in What Matters Most

List your top 5 values and write a vision statement.
Use this compass to guide decisions by checking alignment with your values.

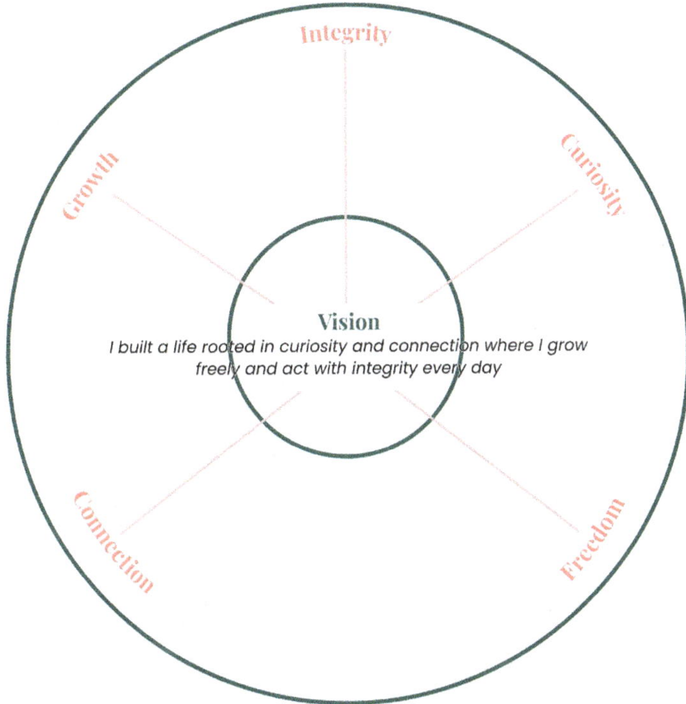

Does this align with what matters most to me?
Does this move me closer to the life I truly want?

CLARITY COMPASS VISUALIZATION (OPTIONAL PROMPT)

Before you write, pause and imagine:

- You are standing at a crossroads.
- One path is lined with pressure, comparison, and self-doubt.
- The other path is lined with your core values steady, peaceful, guiding you forward.

Breathe deeply.

Visualize yourself stepping onto the path that feels aligned with who you really are not who you were told to be.

Ask yourself:

- *What would life feel like if I chose my values every day?*
- *What could I create if I trusted myself more than my fear?*

Let this feeling guide you as you complete your Clarity Compass.

Reflection Prompt:
What would confidence look like if I no longer had anything to prove?

Imagine moving through the world trusting who you are without the need to defend it, explain it, or shrink it.

REFLECTION: MOVING FORWARD

Confidence doesn't come from always being right. It comes from learning how to move with grace through uncertainty.

You don't need to be louder to be more powerful. You don't need to be perfect to be impactful. You don't need permission to own your voice.

Clarity comes when you stop rushing and start listening. And confidence follows when you act from your truth.

Say it now: *I trust myself. I am clear. I am capable.*

Let's build your roadmap.

BONUS INSIGHT: FROM DOUBT TO DECISIVENESS

Many people are surprised to learn that confidence and clarity are not always traits you're born with they are muscles. They are built through repetition, reflection, and practice.

Confidence is also deeply connected to emotional regulation. According to Dr. Susan David, author of *Emotional Agility*

"Courage is not the absence of fear, but fear walking." That is, confident people are not immune to fear they've simply learned how to move with it.

To deepen this practice:

- **Try decision journaling:** Write down what you decided, why, and how it turned out. Over time, you'll see patterns of growing trust in yourself.
- **Name your inner critic:** Give it a silly name to take away its power. Recognize it without obeying it.
- **Share your fears** out loud with a trusted peer or coach. When doubt is voiced, it often loses its grip.

And remember: clarity doesn't mean certainty. It means alignment. If your next step is grounded in your values, it's the right step even if the outcome is unknown.

Growth Is Progress:

You are allowed to grow at your own pace.

You are allowed to change direction when clarity calls you to.

You are allowed to define success by your own values not anyone else's.

Give yourself permission to evolve.

Growth isn't a race; it's a process of strengthening, just like a seed becomes a flower steady, persistent, and unstoppable over time.

Every step you take is still movement forward.

YOUR 5-STEP ROADMAP TO THRIVE

Before we start, here's your full journey at a glance. Think of it like a map—each step builds on the one before it, taking you from where you are now to where you want to be.

YOUR 5 STEP ROADMAP TO THRIVE
A Structured Path for Lasting Growth

Follow the steps from identifying your challenge to celebrating progress, using this roadmap to track steady, purposeful growth.

The 5-Step Roadmap to Thrive (O'Donoghue & Green, 2025)

You've now walked through five deeply personal and profoundly universal challenges. You've read the stories, explored the insights, and gathered tools to support your emotional growth and resilience. Now it's time to bring it all together into a roadmap you can return to again and again as you continue your journey.

This roadmap isn't a rigid prescription. It's a flexible framework designed to meet you where you are, offering guidance, structure, and space for real transformation.

Step 1: Identify Your Core Challenge(s)

You may resonate with all five challenges, or one may stand out right now. Begin by naming which area is currently most active in your life.

- What feels unresolved?
- Which chapter felt the most emotional?
- Where do you feel stuck, avoidant, or overwhelmed?

Start there. Growth begins with awareness.

Step 2: Set SMART Micro Goals

Choose one challenge and define a small, measurable, and compassionate goal related to it. Use the SMART model:

- **Specific**: What exactly do you want to shift?
- **Measurable**: How will you track it?
- **Achievable**: Is this realistic for your energy and life context?
- **Relevant**: Why does this matter to you?
- **Time-Bound**: Set a short time frame (e.g., 7 days or 1 month).

Example: "For the next 7 days, I will write one thing I appreciate about myself every night before bed."

Step 3: Integrate Daily Practice

Change doesn't happen through one big leap it happens in small, consistent steps. Pick one practice from this book to repeat daily:

- A journaling prompt
- A grounding exercise
- A mantra or affirmation
- A morning check-in
- A boundary-setting moment

Integration means making healing part of your everyday life not something you only reach for in crisis.

Step 4: Track & Reflect Weekly

Use a simple tracker (in your journal or a printable template) to note your practices, progress, and emotional shifts.

Weekly Reflection: Turning Actions into Wisdom

Each week, ask yourself:

- What helped me feel more grounded or seen?
- What challenged me, and why?
- What did I learn about myself?
- Was it based on real evidence or just a perspective I had been holding?
- What do I want to shift, strengthen, or let go of next week?

Self-reflection transforms actions into wisdom. It's not just about doing it's about *understanding*.

Step 5: Celebrate & Re-anchor Progress

Growth isn't a straight line and we often forget to acknowledge how far we've come.

Each week and especially at the end of each month take time to honor your progress:

- Write down **5 wins**, big or small.
- Share a reflection with a trusted friend, mentor, or even your future self.
- Revisit your original challenge and notice what has shifted in your thoughts, feelings, or actions.
- Anchor new beliefs by repeating your favorite affirmations daily.

Celebration isn't fluff, its fuel for continued growth.

Learning takes time, patience, and practice.

There will always be days when you need to remind yourself:

- What no longer serves you.
- What you are consciously choosing now.
- How far you've already traveled.

Return to these pages whenever you need.

You are not starting over, you are starting from experience.

REFLECTION: YOU ARE YOUR OWN ANCHOR

You now have a framework you can return to whenever life feels overwhelming, uncertain, or disconnected.

The Power of 5 isn't just a method, it's a movement toward gentler strength, structured support, and meaningful self-discovery.

You are enough.
You are not alone.
You belong.
You are healing.
You are clear and capable.

Let this be your invitation to keep showing up softly, boldly, and intentionally for the life you want to live and the life you deserve.

This is your roadmap.
Now go thrive.

A NOTE FROM
EVELYN & DONNA

If you've made it this far, take a moment to truly acknowledge yourself.
We didn't write this book because we had all the answers, we wrote
it because we've walked through many of these challenges ourselves.
We've sat with the ache of not feeling enough.
We've faced rejection, silence, trauma, and uncertainty.
And we've also experienced the beauty of healing, the strength that
comes from clarity, and the freedom that comes from finally trusting
ourselves.

The Power of 5 is more than a framework.
It's a reflection of our deepest belief: that with the right tools, compassionate support, and a little structure, transformation becomes not
only possible but sustainable.
Healing and growth are not endpoints.

They are journeys of remembering who you are, what you deserve,
and what is possible for you.
If this book has offered you even one moment of clarity, one tool for
comfort, or one reminder that you are not alone, then know this:

You have already begun.

You are already on your way.

There is no perfect timeline. No finish line you must race toward.

There is simply the next step and the next and the next. Let yourself evolve at your own pace.

Let yourself soften into your own becoming.

When you doubt, when you stumble, when you forget, return to these pages.

You are not starting over.

You are starting from experience.

We hope this book has served as a steady companion for your growth offering you stories that resonate, tools that support, and a quiet knowing that you are never truly alone on this path.

Keep showing up for yourself. Keep asking the deeper questions.

Keep allowing yourself to thrive, not just survive.

With all our hearts,

Evelyn & Donna

POETIC REFLECTIONS FROM THE AUTHORS

Two voices.

Two journeys.

One shared belief: that healing is possible, and words can hold space when nothing else can.

These poetic reflections invite you to pause, breathe, and reconnect with your own inner wisdom, whether you're just beginning your healing or honoring how far you've come.

"Becoming"

by Evelyn O'Donoghue

You are not the storm that shook your frame,
Nor the echo lost in someone's name.
You are the breath you fought to find
When chaos tried to cloud your mind.

Not just the shield you learned to raise,
But the whisper within: "I'm still here."
You are the ache, you are the mend,
The fall, the rise, the curve, the bend.

You are not too late, nor too far gone—
You are the dusk that brings the dawn.
So let the past be guide, not chain,
A lesson etched, not carved in pain.
Let softness be the strength you show,

Let steady grace become your glow.
And when it's hard to just keep going,
Pause, feel your breath, and know you're growing.
Place your hand upon your chest—
You're doing your part, you're doing your best.
Say: I am becoming, through light and through rough.
And in this moment, I am enough.

"To the One Who Listens"

by Donna Green

You are the quiet strength in the storm,
The stillness where stories unfold.
Not the one who rushes to fix
But the one who holds.

You carry the weight of unsaid words
With reverence, not fear.
You walk beside the wounded
Until they remember they belong here.

You do not fill the silence
You dignify it.
You do not dim the pain
You witness it, gently inviting light in.

Your presence is a permission
To exhale without apology.
Your eyes say: You are not broken.
Your soul says: You are seen.

So, when the world forgets to pause,
To breathe, to soften, to feel
Let this remind you, dear one: Your way of healing is real.

APPENDIX: ADDITIONAL REFLECTIONS & INSIGHTS

APPENDIX A: WITNESS-BASED TRAUMA

Some trauma isn't experienced directly, but witnessed like seeing a loved one in distress, being present during a crisis, or observing emotional abuse. This is called witness-based trauma.

Because it didn't "happen to you," it often goes unrecognized or invalidated. You may have told yourself, *"I should be fine,"* or *"Others had it worse."* But trauma isn't just about the event itself it's about how the nervous system registers and stores the experience.

Your brain's threat center, the amygdala, cannot distinguish between direct and observed harm. When you witness something disturbing, your body may still respond as if it's happening to you: your heart races, muscles tense, and a sense of danger is logged.

And when that experience is not processed or supported, it can remain stuck in the body, influencing your thoughts, emotions, and behaviors long after the moment has passed.

To complicate matters, others may minimize what you've been through:

"At least it wasn't you."
"You're strong you'll get over it."

This kind of response can deepen shame, increase emotional withdrawal, and delay healing.

Common Symptoms of Witness-Based Trauma:

- Recurring mental images or flashbacks of what you saw
- Emotional detachment or numbness, especially during downtime
- Avoidance of similar environments, conversations, or media
- Heightened irritability or startle response
- Internal guilt: *"Why didn't I do more?"* or *"Why does this still affect me?"*

Long-Term Impact:

If left unresolved, witness-based trauma may contribute to:

- Anxiety and hypervigilance
- Relational withdrawal or shutdown
- Difficulty regulating under stress
- Reduced emotional availability
- Symptoms of burnout or persistent unease

These effects can ripple into your work, relationships, and sense of safety even if you appear "fine" on the outside.

Healing Philosophy:

Healing does not mean you're broken.

It means you're integrating what you've witnessed, felt, and absorbed so that it no longer runs silently in the background of your life.

This isn't about weakness. It's about building inner safety.

You don't need to override your nervous system you need to listen to it.

By creating intentional space to reflect, feel, and restore, you give yourself permission to be both strong *and* supported.

Tools for Support & Integration:

- **Emotional Journaling Prompt:** *"What did I witness that shifted something in me?* "Let yourself write freely without editing or minimizing.
- **Co-Regulation Strategies:** Engage in safe, calming experiences with others (e.g., grounding conversations, shared breathwork, or calming physical presence).
- **Psychoeducation:** Learn how trauma responses show up in the body even when the event was not your own. Understanding the science helps reduce shame and normalize what you're feeling.
- **Professional Support:** Consider seeking guidance from a qualified counsellor or coach who can help you process and integrate these experiences safely.

APPENDIX B: NATURAL DISASTERS AND ENVIRONMENTAL TRIGGERS

Understanding How Unpredictable Events
Impact Emotional Safety and Recovery

Environmental trauma doesn't always make the headlines but it can live on quietly, deeply, and disruptively within the nervous system of those who experience it.

For individuals who are usually organized, capable, and proactive, the unpredictability of natural disasters strikes at the very core of what they work hard to maintain: **safety, structure, and control**.

You may logically know that the storm has passed yet emotionally, your body keeps preparing for the next one.

This is known as **anticipatory fear.**

The nervous system braces months ahead, long before the weather changes, triggered by a shift in the wind, a news alert, or even the low rumble of distant thunder.

For driven individuals who depend on structure and preparation, it can feel especially disorienting when external forces threaten your internal sense of stability.

And when the home the usual place of refuge feels vulnerable or violated, the nervous system may remain activated long after the physical danger is gone.

Key Emotional Themes:

- **Anticipatory Fear:** Subtle dread that builds in the body as storm seasons approach, even when there is no immediate threat.

- **Sensory-Based Trauma:** Anxiety spikes triggered by rainstorms, sirens, flickering lights, heavy winds, or sudden power outages.

- **Chronic Vigilance:** Hyperawareness of surroundings, constantly scanning for safety threats even after events have ended.

- **Emotional Displacement:** Difficulty acknowledging your own fear, grief, or losses because others "had it worse" or because you feel you "should be fine."

Long-Term Impact of Unaddressed Environmental Trauma

When environmental trauma remains unprocessed, it can manifest in various ways:

- **Sleep disturbances:** Insomnia, frequent nightmares, or restless sleep patterns.

- **Somatic symptoms:** Chronic tension, unexplained pain, or gastrointestinal issues.

- **Emotional dysregulation:** Heightened anxiety, irritability, or emotional shutdown.

- **Relationship strain:** Withdrawal from loved ones, difficulty trusting stability, fear of future unpredictability.

- **Hypervigilance:** Constant scanning for danger, even in safe environments.

- **Generalized anxiety:** Persistent underlying unease, especially during environmental changes like seasonal shifts or storms.

The body's nervous system does not easily distinguish between *real danger* and *remembered danger* unless we consciously introduce intentional cues of safety and practice nervous system regulation.

Healing Approach

Healing isn't about ignoring the very real threats you have survived.

It's about teaching your body that safety is possible again even when reminders of the past arise.

For individuals who thrive on structure and action, integrating deliberate rituals and organized supports into your healing process can feel especially empowering and stabilizing.

Tools to Reclaim Safety and Stability:

- **Create a Calm Kit:** Assemble sensory comfort items (e.g., a soft blanket, calming essential oils, a weighted eye mask, soothing playlists) that you can access during stress spikes.
- **Develop an Emergency Emotional Plan (EEP):** Write out calming strategies, safe contacts, grounding exercises, and reminders to use when triggered. Treat this plan like you would a physical emergency kit accessible and prepared ahead of time.
- **Reclaim Positive Weather Rituals:** Create new, safe associations with weather patterns.
  - Example: *Write poetry while it rains.*
  - Example: *Light a candle and journal during thunder-storms.* These rituals rewire sensory memories by layering positive experiences over old fear patterns.

APPENDIX C: SUCCESS, COMPARISON & MILESTONES

When Achievement Isn't Enough

Many driven individuals grow up linking their self-worth to external accomplishments.

Success becomes the measure of value:

- Praise comes after winning.
- Love is easier to believe after achievement.
- Belonging is granted after proving yourself.

But what happens when you hit the milestone and it doesn't fill the emptiness?

This experience is called the Milestone Drop: a moment of confusion, sadness, or emptiness after achieving something you worked so hard for.

It's not a sign of failure.

It's a signal that external achievements cannot fulfill internal needs.

Psychological Impact:

- Self-worth tied to productivity, status, or recognition
- Chronic comparison to others' highlight reels
- Fear that slowing down means losing value
- Loss of joy when there's nothing left to "achieve" immediately

Healing Approach:

Healing from milestone-related emptiness doesn't mean giving up ambition.

It means reclaiming your intrinsic worth the part of you that matters even when you're not producing, winning, or performing.

Your value is not earned. It is remembered.

Tools for Breaking the Cycle:

- Joy Anchor List: Identify 10 small daily pleasures that have nothing to do with achievement. (Examples: Morning sunlight, a deep breath, a favorite song.)
- Social Media Detox & Reflection: Take short breaks from comparison-based platforms. Journal: What parts of my life feel most real when I'm not measuring them against others?
- Transitioning Rituals: Before and after completing major goals, pause to affirm: "I am proud because I exist, not because I perform. This helps release the hidden weight of "having it all."

APPENDIX D: IDENTITY, DEPRESSION & HIGH ACHIEVEMENT

For many high achievers, success on the outside can act as armor, shielding profound struggle on the inside.

You accomplish more and yet feel more isolated.

- You meet goals and yet wonder, *Is this all there is?*
- You lead others and yet feel unseen yourself.

This dissonance can create a unique form of emotional exhaustion. It's not simply burnout it's a loss of connection to self.

Emotional Landscape:

- Internalized pressure to never slow down
- Fear that stillness equals irrelevance or failure
- Guilt for feeling dissatisfied after achieving success
- Survivor's guilt: *"Why me, when others struggle?"*

Expanding Understanding:

Post-Traumatic Stress Response (PTSR)

Not all emotional pain fits neatly into clinical diagnoses. Some individuals experience profound symptoms hypervigilance, emotional shutdown, restlessness not because they are "disordered," but because their nervous system has been in prolonged survival mode.

By using terms like Post-Traumatic Stress Response (PTSR), we honor emotional suffering without automatically labeling it a disorder while also acknowledging that, for some, clinical support is essential and validating.

Both realities can be true.

Healing Approach:

Healing success-related depression or exhaustion requires reclaiming identity outside of achievement.
You are not just what you do.
You are who you are becoming.
You deserve fulfillment not just accomplishment.

Tools for Emotional Reconnection:

- **Self-Worth Redefinition:** Write a statement: *"I am worthy because I exist not because I perform."*
  Post it somewhere visible as a daily reminder.
- **Reflective Prompts:**
  - *What does success mean to me now?*
  - *What parts of myself am I ready to honor that have nothing to do with results?*
- **Self-Compassion Statements and Mood Check-Ins:** Build daily rituals where you check in not just on tasks completed, but on how you feel and what you need.

APPENDIX E: CULTURAL & GENERATIONAL TRAUMA

Understanding Emotional Inheritance and Conscious Healing

Our emotional blueprint often begins long before we do.

We inherit not only physical features but also deeply in-grained beliefs about love, rest, ambition, worth, and emotional expression from the families, communities, and cultures we are born into.

Cultural and generational trauma isn't always a single event it's often the subtle, repeated emotional norms we absorb without even realizing it.

In many households and societies:

- Strength is valued over vulnerability.

- Work is praised more than play.
- Independence is encouraged at the expense of asking for help.

These emotional codes shape not just how we behave, but how we view ourselves and the world.

You may have heard messages like:

- *"Don't cry. Be strong."*
- *"We don't talk about those things."*
- *"You have to work twice as hard to be seen."*
- *"I had it much worse. You should be grateful."*

While these lessons may have been passed down with love or survival in mind they can still leave lasting emotional imprints.

They can influence:

- How you express needs (or suppress them)
- How you handle conflict (with silence or overcompensation)
- How you view rest, joy, self-worth, and emotional safety

Important Note:

Healing cultural and generational trauma is not about assigning blame.

It's about gaining understanding recognizing the emotional legacies you carry and consciously choosing, where possible, to do things differently.

You honor your ancestors not just by repeating their survival patterns, but also by evolving them.

Tools for Healing Cultural & Generational Patterns:

Family Belief Mapping: Write down five core emotional beliefs you absorbed during your upbringing.

- Which beliefs supported your growth?
- Which ones now feel limiting or outdated? Reframe each one according to your own conscious value system.

Reflection Prompts:

- *Which inherited beliefs truly serve me today?*
- *Which beliefs am I ready to release or transform into something healthier?*
- *What new beliefs would I choose to pass forward?*

Honor Ancestral Resilience: Recognize that survival required strength, adaptability, and courage. Your growth does not dishonor your past it fulfills the deeper dream of those who came before you: that each generation might have more freedom, more safety, and more emotional wholeness

APPENDIX F: NAVIGATING CHANGE WHILE HEALING

Staying Grounded During Emotional and Life Transitions

We often begin our healing work right when something in life is shifting a new job, a breakup, a move, or an internal realization that we're no longer aligned with how things used to be.

Healing and change often arrive hand-in-hand.

While that can be a powerful catalyst, it can also feel overwhelming.

In these moments, your nervous system carries a dual load processing both past experiences and present uncertainty.

This can lead to emotional fatigue, indecision, or a sense of paralysis.

Part of you may feel excited to grow, while another part clings to the safety of the familiar.

This inner tension isn't a sign of failure.

It's a natural part of transformation and it's known as mental resistance.

Common Emotional Responses to Change:

- Grieving your former self (even when moving toward something better)
- Missing the confidence that came with predictability
- Feeling unanchored without clear roles, routines, or external validation
- Experiencing fear about stepping into a new version of yourself without guarantees

Identity shifts especially those tied to purpose, relationships, or self-worth can leave you feeling like you're floating between two worlds.

That feeling is part of the path. Not a detour. Not a mistake.

Tools for Navigating Change with Grace:

- **Change Tolerance Timeline:** Track your emotional highs and lows during recent changes. Map out the supportive structures (people, rituals, self-care) you have and identify any gaps you want to strengthen.
- **Stability Anchors:** Choose three grounding rituals to consistently return to when you feel overwhelmed. *Examples:* Morning tea without screens, a daily 10-minute walk, journaling three emotions without judgment.
- **Self-Permission Practice:** Remind yourself daily:
  - It's okay to move slowly.
  - It's okay to not know yet.
  - It's okay to pause and breathe before the next step.

Offer yourself the same grace you would offer someone you love.

Healing and growth are not measured in speed they're measured in presence, courage, and self-compassion.

Reflection: Honoring Growth During Change

Before you move forward, take a quiet moment to reflect:

- *What parts of me am I ready to honor during this season of change?*
- *What old habits or beliefs am I ready to thank and gently release?*
- *Where can I offer myself more grace as I grow into something new?*

There is no rush.
You are not falling behind.
You are becoming.

APPENDIX G: ADDICTION AND EMOTIONAL TRAUMA

When Coping Becomes Survival,
and Survival Leaves a Mark

Trauma doesn't always come from a single event.

Sometimes, it stems from living within an environment shaped by **addiction** whether it's your own, a parent's, a partner's, or another close family member's.

When addiction is present in a household, emotional safety becomes unpredictable.

Even if no explicit harm was intended, the emotional residue of addiction chaos, hypervigilance, secrecy, shame can leave lasting imprints on the nervous system.

How Addiction Becomes Trauma:

- **Emotional Unavailability:** Caregivers struggling with addiction may be physically present but emotionally absent, creating feelings of abandonment.
- **Unpredictability:** Moods, behavior, and stability shift without warning. This leads to chronic stress and hyper-alertness.
- **Silencing and Shame:** Many families operate under unspoken rules like, "Don't talk about it," or "Pretend everything is fine," causing emotional isolation.
- **Role Reversal:** Children may take on adult responsibilities far too early becoming mediators, caregivers, or emotional support systems.

- **Internalized Guilt or Control:** You may believe it was your job to keep things stable, and if you failed, it was your fault.

Lasting Impact:

- People-pleasing, perfectionism, or difficulty trusting others
- Fear of emotional intimacy or being "too much"
- Deep feelings of shame, guilt, or emotional disconnection
- Self-blame and hyper-responsibility in adulthood
- Struggles with boundaries, conflict avoidance, or dissociation

You may have learned to **over-function** to survive becoming the "responsible one," the "achiever," or the "peacekeeper."

These patterns are not character flaws. They are adaptations.

Tools for Healing Addiction-Related Trauma:

- **Family Systems Reflection** Write out the emotional "rules" you absorbed in your family (e.g., *Don't feel. Don't trust. Don't need.*) Ask: *Which of these still serve me and which ones can I release?*
- **Inner Child Reassurance** Affirm to yourself regularly: *"It wasn't my job to fix anyone. I am safe now. "*Use journaling to write messages of support to the younger version of you.
- **Boundary and Safety Mapping** Identify 23 ways to create emotional safety in your current life:(Trusted people, safe spaces, rituals, language like "That's not mine to carry.")
- **Naming What Was True** You don't need permission to name what you experienced. It matters even if it wasn't "as bad" as someone else's story. If it impacted you, it matters.

A Note on Professional Support

If you or someone you love is currently impacted by addiction, please know that addiction therapy especially for families is a highly specialized field.

We strongly encourage you to seek out a qualified addiction-focused therapist or family support professional who understands the complex dynamics involved.

Healing is possible but it often requires the right kind of support.

You are not alone.

You were never meant to carry it all by yourself.

APPENDIX H: DIVORCE, SEPARATION & REDEFINING IDENTITY

When the Story Changes, But You Still Belong in It

Divorce or separation can feel like a personal earthquake shaking your foundation, disrupting your sense of identity, and reshaping everything from daily life to long-term dreams.

Even when a breakup is chosen, mutual, or "for the best," the emotional aftermath can carry grief, guilt, fear, and a deep sense of disorientation.

Who am I without this relationship?
What does family look like now?
Will I be okay on my own?

Why This Is Trauma (Even If No One Talks About It)

Separation is not just the ending of a relationship it's the ending of a vision. It's a disruption to belonging, safety, routine, and in many cases, identity.

The nervous system doesn't distinguish between emotional pain and physical threat it simply registers loss, uncertainty and vulnerability.

Common emotional responses may include:

- Shame ("Why couldn't I make it work?")
- Guilt (especially when children are involved)
- Anxiety about the future or finances
- Loneliness, even in moments of relief
- Identity grief ("I don't know who I am anymore.")

These are not signs of weakness. They are human responses to deep disruption.

Tools for Healing After Separation

- **Relationship Reflection Letter** Write a letter to your former partner (you won't send it). Name what hurt. Name what helped. Name what you're letting go of.
- **Role Identity Inventory** List roles you carried in the relationship (e.g., caregiver, peacekeeper, fixer). Ask: *Which ones still feel true to me now? Which ones can I release?*
- **Self-Reclamation Ritual** Choose one small act each week that reconnects you to *you*. Examples: solo travel, sleeping diagonally in your bed, updating your space, reclaiming your voice through journaling or movement.

- **Affirmation Practice** Repeat: *"I am whole even in this in-between. I am allowed to grieve and grow at the same time."*
- **Support Map** Identify your current support system: friends, therapists, coaches, groups. If the circle feels small, consider reaching out or joining community spaces where healing is normalized.

Gentle Reminder:

The end of a relationship does not mean the end of your worth.

You are allowed to redefine what love, family, and success mean to you now.

You are allowed to feel sad, strong, confused, and hopeful all in the same breath.

You are still becoming. And you are not alone.

REFERENCES

Brown, B. (2012). *Daring greatly: How the courage to be vulnerable transforms the way we live, love, parent, and lead.* Avery.

Brown, B. (2017). *Braving the wilderness: The quest for true belonging and the courage to stand alone.* Random House.

Bryant-Davis, T. (2011). *Thriving in the wake of trauma: A multicultural guide.* Praeger.

David, S. (2016). *Emotional agility: Get unstuck, embrace change, and thrive in work and life.* Avery.

Doran, G. T. (1981). There's a S.M.A.R.T. way to write management's goals and objectives. *Management Review, 70*(11), 35–36.

Dweck, C. S. (2006). *Mindset: The new psychology of success.* Random House.

Levine, P. A. (1997). *Waking the tiger: Healing trauma.* North Atlantic Books.

Maté, G. (2003). *When the body says no: Understanding the stress-disease connection.* Wiley.

O'Donoghue, E., & Green, D. (2025). *The power of 5: Overcoming life's biggest challenges to thrive.* Self-published.

van der Kolk, B. A. (2014). *The body keeps the score: Brain, mind, and body in the healing of trauma.* Penguin Books.

COMPANION WORKBOOK: THE POWER OF 5

Introduction: How to Use This Workbook

This workbook is designed to help you apply the insights and tools from *The Power of 5: Overcoming Life's Biggest Challenges to Thrive.*

Each section corresponds with one of the five emotional challenges discussed in the book and is structured to support clarity, integration, and personal growth.

Each chapter includes:

- Guided journal prompts
- Tool-based activities
- Reflection visualizations
- Tracking sheets
- Intention-setting spaces
- Breathing and grounding practices

You can move through it chapter by chapter, revisit exercises weekly, or return to certain sections whenever you need extra support.

Chapter 1: Am I Enough? Overcoming Self-Worth Blocks

Journal Prompts

- *When did you first feel you needed to earn love or praise? Pay attention to whose voice you hear is it truly yours?*
- *What are five non-performance-based qualities you appreciate about yourself?*

Exercises

- **Self-Worth Inventory:** List 10 traits that make you valuable beyond achievement.
- **Reframe Worksheet:** Write three negative beliefs and transform them into self-compassionate affirmations.
- **Chart Your Experiences: Self-Esteem vs. Self-Worth:** Reflect on key life events that shaped your beliefs about yourself.

Tracker

- **Gratitude for Self-Tracker (7 Days):** Log one thing you appreciate about yourself each day.
- **Daily Affirmation Practice:** "I am enough because I exist."

Chapter 2: Abandoned & Neglected - Healing Disconnection

Journal Prompts

- *When do you feel most unseen or unimportant?*
- *What memories surface when you think about being left out?*

Exercises

- **Circle of Trust Map:** Identify emotionally safe people and what qualities make you feel seen.
- **Inner Child Letter:** Write a compassionate letter to your younger self offering love, guidance, and safety.
- **Self-Soothing Toolkit:** List 5 personal comfort strategies.
- **Boundary & Reconnection Scripts:** Practice boundary-setting phrases and morning reconnection rituals (including 4-4-6 breathing).

Chapter 3: Do I Belong? Navigating Social Anxiety

Journal Prompts

- *When do you feel like you don't belong?*
- *How do you protect yourself in groups?*

Exercises

- **Belonging Statement:** Identify your unique qualities and affirm your worthiness of connection.
- **Social Exposure Ladder:** Create a step-by-step list of social risks to build confidence.
- **Weekly Social Reflection Ritual:** Where did you show up authentically this week?

Chapter 4: Big T & Little t-Reframing Painful Experiences

Journal Prompts

- *What's one painful memory that still carries emotional charge?*
- *What do you need to believe about yourself to reframe that story?*

Exercises

- **Trauma Triggers Map:** Track recurring emotional patterns back to early roots.
- **Grounding Sequence:** 5-4-3-2-1 sensory grounding technique.
- **Rewrite the Story Practice:** Retell a painful event with compassion and empowerment.
- **Somatic Tracking Exercise:** 4-4-6 breathing and gentle body scans.
- **Personalized Self-Care Plan:** Build a toolkit of rituals, grounding tools, and daily affirmations.

Chapter 5: Confidence & Clarity Moving Beyond Emotional Hurdles

Journal Prompts

- *Where in your life do you second-guess yourself the most?*
- *What does clarity feel like in your body?*

Exercises

- Confidence Wins Tracker: Log small moments of bravery, honesty, and decisiveness.
- Clarity Compass Mapping:
- Identify top 5 core values.
- Write a one-sentence vision statement.
- Use visualization to imagine living by your values daily.

Reflection Prompts

What would confidence look like if I no longer had anything to prove?

Final Section: 5-Step Roadmap to Thrive

Step 1: Identify Your Challenge

- Reflection page: Explore your current core emotional challenge.

Step 2: Set SMART Micro Goals

- SMART Goal Planning Sheet: Break goals into manageable steps.

Step 3: Integrate Daily Practice

- Habit Builder Template: Commit to one practice for 21 days.

Step 4: Weekly Reflection

- Weekly Reflection Questions:
  - What helped me feel grounded?

- What challenged me, and why?
- What did I learn about myself fact or perspective?
- What do I want to shift next week?

Step 5: Celebrate and Re-anchor Progress

- Progress Milestone Sheet: 5 wins per month.
- Celebration Journal: "What am I proud of today?"
- Affirmation Anchor: Repeat daily affirmations to sustain growth.

Closing Intention Statement

Take a moment to capture your personal commitment moving forward. This statement is your anchor — something you can revisit when you need clarity, reassurance, or motivation.

Steps to Create Your Statement:

1. **Reflect:** What do you most want to release? (e.g., self-doubt, comparison, proving yourself)
2. **Embrace:** What do you most want to welcome? (e.g., confidence, ease, clarity, self-trust)
3. **Phrase:** Turn it into a short mantra, a visual cue, or a single sentence. Keep it simple and memorable.

Example:

- *"I choose clarity over confusion."*
- *"I am rooted in my worth."*
- *"I no longer chase; I allow."*

FURTHER READING & RESOURCES

(Curated for readers who want to explore deeper. Each category is divided into timeless classics that remain foundational, and recent insights offering fresh perspectives.)

Books

Timeless Classics

- **Neff, K. (2011).** *Self-compassion.* **William Morrow.**
  → Foundational guide to self-compassion and reducing self-criticism.
- **Brown, B. (2010).** *The gifts of imperfection.* **Hazelden.**
  → A call to embrace authenticity over perfection.
- **van der Kolk, B. A. (2014).** *The body keeps the score.* **Penguin Books.**
  → Landmark work on trauma and healing through integration.

Recent Insights (2020-2025)

- Gervais, M. (2023). *The First Rule of Mastery.* HarperOne.
  → Framework for breaking free from external validation.
- Khazan, O. (2025). *Me, But Better.* Crown.
  → Explores how intentional change reshapes personality and self-perception.
- Menswar, B. (2020). *Black Sheep: Unleash the Extraordinary, Awe-Inspiring, Undiscovered You.*
  → A guide to discovering and honoring your non-negotiables to live authentically.

Podcasts

Timeless Classics

- **Unlocking Us with Brené Brown**
  → Conversations on vulnerability, courage, and connection.
- **On Being with Krista Tippett**
  → Thoughtful dialogue on meaning and belonging.
- **The Trauma Therapist Podcast (Guy Macpherson, PhD)**
  → Foundational discussions on trauma and healing.

Recent Insights (2023–2025)

- *The Homecoming Podcast with Dr. Thema Bryant*
  → Soulful, culturally rooted tools for healing and belonging.
- *Pulling the Thread with Elise Loehnen*
  → Explores modern dilemmas of worth, meaning, and balance.
- *Just a Moment with Brant Menswar*
  → High-achieving guests share breakthrough and missed moments, highlighting the power of pivotal life experiences.

Films & Documentaries

Timeless Classics

- **Inside Out (2015, Pixar)**
  → Creative introduction to emotional awareness.
- **The Wisdom of Trauma (2021)**
  → Dr. Gabor Maté on how trauma shapes lives and how compassion heals.
- **Heal (2017)**
  → Examines the mind-body connection in healing.

Recent Insights (2023–2025)

- **Stutz (2022, Netflix)**
  → Jonah Hill's intimate portrait of therapy tools for growth.
- **Live to 100: Secrets of the Blue Zones (2023, Netflix)**
  → Lessons on resilience and thriving across cultures.
- **The Deepest Breath (2023, Netflix)**
  → Explores courage, risk, and pushing human limits.

FINAL NOTE & NEXT STEPS

Additional Support

If this book has resonated with you and you're ready to continue your journey, Evelyn and Donna offer ways to help you deepen your growth, gain clarity, and move forward with purpose.

Evelyn O'Donoghue – Purisoul Wellbeing

Founder of Purisoul Wellbeing, Evelyn offers:

- Self-paced programs for clarity, emotional alignment, and sustainable success
- *The Power of 5 Companion* Coaching Journey
- 1:1 Strategic Clarity & Action Sessions
  Visit: **www.purisoulwellbeing.com/programs**

Donna Green – Harmony Wellness Coaching

Founder of Harmony Wellness Coaching, Donna offers:

- Health & wellness coaching for emotional resilience and self-worth
- The Power of 5 Companion Coaching Journey
- 1:1 Reflective Growth & Support Sessions
  Visit: **www.harmonywellnesscoaching.org**

"The Power of Five"
Five Core Challenges That Shape Our Inner World

Use this framework to explore which challenge resonates most with your own experience—it may be one, or several, at different times.

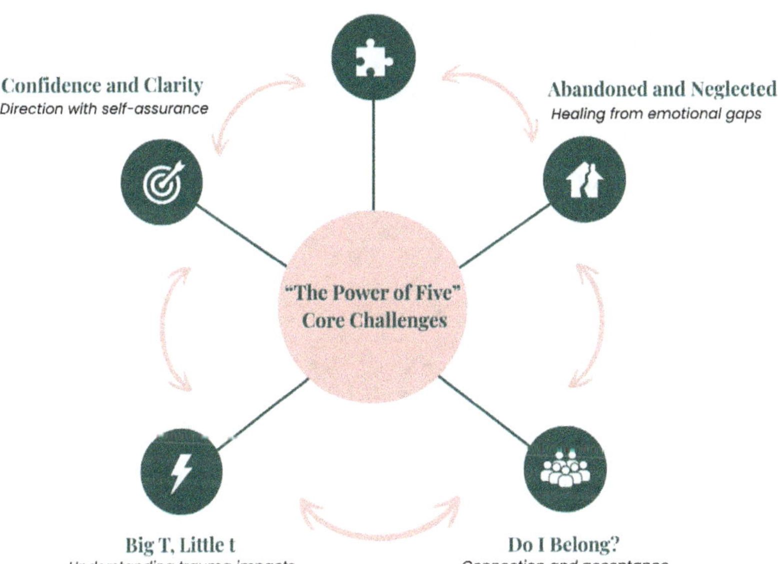

The 5 Core Challenges Framework (O'Donoghue & Green, 2025)